Tree
of Life

The Incredible
Biodiversity of
Life on Earth

WRITTEN BY
Rochelle Strauss

ILLUSTRATED BY
Margot Thompson

KIDS CAN PRESS

For Oliver and Rosanne, with much love.

Acknowledgments

My deepest thanks to Valerie Hussey and Valerie Wyatt, whose faith and wisdom guided me in bringing
this idea to life. Much gratitude as well to Margot Thompson for her breathtaking illustrations and
Marie Bartholomew for crafting together concepts, words and images in such a beautiful way. Thanks
also to Susan, Liz and Kate, for making me laugh when the numbers became overwhelming, and to Julia
for helping me believe in my true calling as an "otter." Big hugs to my family, for their love and support.
And a very special thank you to Rosanne, for constantly daring me to make my dreams come true.

Of course, this book would not have been possible without my intrepid team of technical reviewers:
Joanne DiCosimo, Mark Graham and Robert Anderson, Canadian Museum of Nature; Ann Jarnet,
Environment Canada; Liz Lundy, World Wildlife Fund; and Susan Gesner, Gesner & Associates
Environmental Learning. Special thanks to them for their valuable input and insight.

A note on species and numbers

The sheer magnitude of biodiversity on Earth means that scientists do not know the exact numbers
of species between and within the five kingdoms. The figures used in this book are based on their
best estimates and have been rounded up or down to make them more manageable. The ellipsis (...)
used in the species lists indicate that listed species are examples from a larger group.

Kids Can Press acknowledges the financial support of the
Government of Ontario, through the Ontario Media
Development Corporation's Ontario Book Initiative; the
Ontario Arts Council; the Canada Council for the Arts;
and the Government of Canada, through the BPIDP, for
our publishing activity.

Published in Canada by
Kids Can Press Ltd.
29 Birch Avenue
Toronto, ON M4V 1E2

Published in the U.S. by
Kids Can Press Ltd.
2250 Military Road
Tonawanda, NY 14150

www.kidscanpress.com

Edited by Valerie Wyatt
Designed by Marie Bartholomew
Printed and bound in Hong Kong, China,
by Book Art Inc., Toronto

This book is smyth sewn casebound.

CM 04 0 9 8 7 6 5 4 3 2

National Library of Canada Cataloguing in Publication Data

Strauss, Rochelle, 1967–
Tree of life : the incredible biodiversity of life on earth / Rochelle
Strauss ; illustrated by Margot Thompson.

Includes index.
ISBN 1-55337-669-2

1. Biology — Classification — Juvenile literature. 2. Biological
diversity — Juvenile literature. I. Thompson, Margot, 1965–
II. Title.

QH541.15.B56S77 2004   j578'.01'2   C2003-906688-6

Kids Can Press is a CORUS™ Entertainment company

Contents

The Tree of Life

Do you have a family tree that shows how the members of your family—aunts, cousins, grandparents and so on—are related?

```
                        Grandma
        ┌──────────┬──────────────┬──────────────┐
    Aunt Sue   Uncle Liam        Mom        Aunt Serina
   ┌─────┴─────┐              ┌────┼────┐
Cousin Rob  Cousin Maria     Me  Louis  Heidi
```

The Tree of Life is like a family tree for all living things. It shows us *biodiversity*, the incredible variety of life on Earth. And it shows us how all living things—from bacteria too small to see with the naked eye to the largest mammal, the blue whale—are related.

So far, scientists have discovered and named 1 750 000 different species (groups of living things that share similar characteristics). If each species were represented by a leaf, there would be 1 750 000 leaves on the Tree of Life.* And all those leaves would be related, some closely on the same branch, others more distantly.

Each part of the Tree of Life is important. A problem with one branch, one twig or even just one leaf may affect the whole tree. Perhaps by climbing the Tree of Life and exploring its branches, we will come to better understand our place within the Tree of Life and our impact on it.

*Note: Scientists do not agree on the exact numbers of species—there are just too many to be sure. The numbers in this book are based on their best estimates.

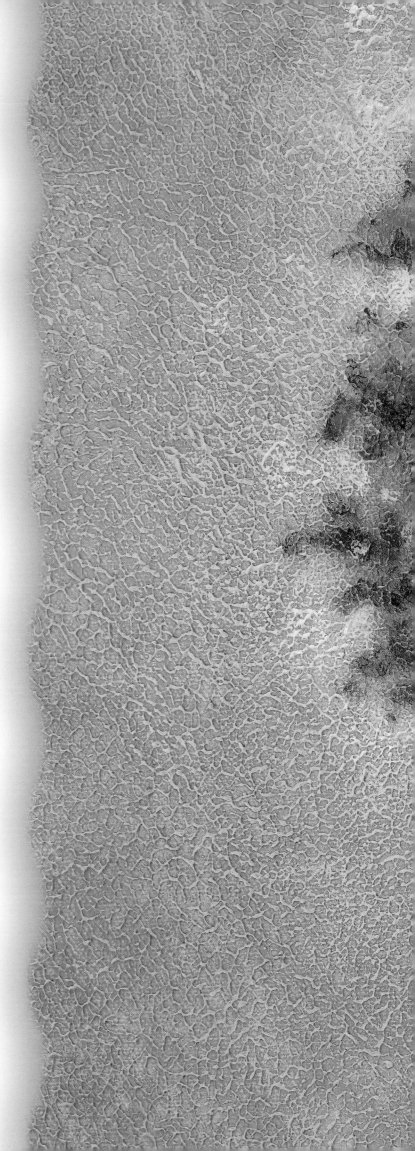

The Five Branches

The Tree of Life is a way to organize, or "classify," all life. By organizing living things into different branches, we can better understand how closely—or distantly—they are related.

The Tree of Life is often divided into five main branches called "kingdoms."

Kingdom Monera
bacteria

Kingdom Fungi
mushrooms, yeasts, lichens …

Kingdom Protoctista
paramecia, amoebas, algae …

Kingdom Plants
flowering plants, mosses, ferns …

Kingdom Animals
from invertebrates such as sponges and spiders to vertebrates such as fish, birds, reptiles, amphibians and mammals

Each kingdom on the Tree of Life has a story to tell us about biodiversity and life on Earth.

Cyanobacteria are not only the oldest known bacteria, they are also the most important to life on Earth. Over 3.5 billion years ago, the first cyanobacteria began to create the oxygen that eventually allowed for other life on Earth to exist.

Do you like beans? Or peas? Without bacteria, such as *Rhizobium*, these legumes — and many other plants — couldn't survive. Some bacteria live in the roots of plants and help the plants get the nutrients they need to survive.

Rhizobium

Cyanobacteria

Lactrobacillus acidophilus

KINGDOM
Monera
10 000 species

You can't see them, but they're out there — the 10 000 species of bacteria that make up the Kingdom Monera.

Bacteria are the smallest life forms on Earth. They are made up of just a single cell and are so tiny that 1000 of them would fit on the period at the end of this sentence. They're everywhere — on land, in water, even inside you. And there may be hundreds of thousands more to be discovered, including in the harshest environments on Earth — hot springs, sea vents and areas deep beneath the soil.

The Kingdom Monera accounts for less than 1 percent of all species on the Tree of Life, but it is still an important kingdom. It contains the oldest living species. Fossils reveal that bacteria have been around for more than 3.5 billion years. These ancient bacteria were the *basis* of all life on Earth.

We sometimes think of bacteria only as carriers of disease, but bacteria are much more than that. Every living thing on the Tree of Life has descended from the early bacteria.

There are billions of bacteria in your intestines. One of them, *Lactobacillus acidophilus*, helps protect you from harmful bacteria.

Monera — 10 000 leaves on the Tree of Life

KINGDOM
Fungi
72 000 species

Is there a fungus among us? Chances are pretty good that you've seen or even eaten one today. Every time you bite into a piece of bread, you are eating yeast, a species of fungus. Scientists believe that as many as one million more fungi species have yet to be discovered.

Some fungi are *parasitic*—they grow on other living plants and animals and get their nutrients from them. But most fungi are *decomposers*—they get nutrients from dead plants or animals. Decomposers are the recyclers and cleaners on the Tree of Life.

Imagine a forest in the fall, with billions of leaves falling to the ground. Where does all this "litter" go? Fungi (and some bacteria) help break it down and absorb it as food. And as they do, they create carbon dioxide, which plants use to make their own food.

Without fungi, the Tree of Life would become buried under its own litter.

Fungi species

30 000 sac fungi (truffles, morels, yeast, lichen ...)

22 250 club fungi (mushrooms, toadstools, puffballs ...)

17 000 imperfect fungi (penicillin, candida ...)

600 conjugation fungi (black bread molds ...)

... and others

Fungi — 72 000 leaves on the Tree of Life

Lichens absorb toxins (poisons) from their environment. When lichens in an area start dying, it's an early warning signal that pollution levels may be high.

The world's oldest and heaviest fungus is an *Armillaria bulbosa* that lives beneath a forest floor in Michigan. This 1500-year-old fungus may be far heavier than an African elephant, but all that's visible are its tiny shoots poking up above the ground.

The smallest puffball fungus is about the size of a chicken egg. The biggest is the size of a watermelon.

British soldier lichen

Armillaria bulbosa

Most protoctista are microscopic, but some, such as seaweed and kelp, can be huge. The largest, the Pacific giant kelp, can grow up to 65 m (213 ft.) in length — as long as five school buses parked end to end. Kelp provides shelter for marine animals.

Paramecia, a type of protozoa, have tiny hairlike structures called cilia. To help paramecia move in their watery habitats, the cilia move back and forth — a little like rowing a boat.

The ocean's largest animal, the blue whale, feeds on its tiniest inhabitants, plankton.

Have you ever seen the surface of the ocean shimmer at night? You may be seeing fire algae, which produce light through bioluminescence, a chemical reaction.

Giant kelp

Plankton

Fire algae

KINGDOM
Protoctista
80 000 species

Paramecia

Are they plants? Animals? The answer is yes ... and no. The Kingdom Protoctista has a little bit of everything. Some species (the algae) are plantlike — they can make their own food. Others (the protozoa) are animal-like — they depend on other species for food.

Protoctista are found in water and other wet environments. In the ocean, they are a major food source known as plankton. Fish, shrimp and other crustaceans eat plankton and in turn become food for other animals, both in water and on land. This is called a food chain. When many food chains are linked together, they form a food web. Without plankton, many species would starve, and the food webs that support the Tree of Life might break down.

Algae have another important role. They help maintain the balance of gases in Earth's atmosphere. How? Algae, like plants, absorb carbon dioxide and use sunlight to create food for themselves. (This process is called photosynthesis.) By doing so, they also create the oxygen that all animals on the Tree of Life need to breathe.

Protoctista species

55 000 protozoa
(paramecia, amoebas ...)

25 000 algae
(green algae, red algae, fire algae ...)

Protoctista — 80 000 leaves on the Tree of Life

13

KINGDOM

Plants

270 000 species

Just about anywhere you look on land, you will find members of the plant kingdom. They range from the flowers in your window box, to the trees that give you shade in the summer, to the mosses you walk on in the woods and the veggies you eat for dinner.

Plants provide valuable habitats for many animals. A habitat is an area where species can find the food, shelter, water and space they need to survive. Without habitats, animals could not survive.

Like protoctista, plants are also at the base of food chains. Plants make their own food — and become food for other living things. A rabbit nibbles on a clover plant. A snake eats the rabbit, then a hawk eats the snake. When the hawk dies, bacteria and fungi feed on its body. Without plants, food chains and webs on the Tree of Life would collapse, and species would become extinct.

As plants make food for themselves during photosynthesis, they create oxygen. Next time you take a deep breath (or even just a tiny one), remember that the oxygen plants produce makes life on Earth possible.

Plant species

235 000 flowering plants (maples, oaks, cacti, grasses, daisies ...)

12 000 ferns (maidenhair fern, Boston fern, staghorn fern ...)

10 000 mosses (peat moss, sphagnum moss, granite moss ...)

630 conifers (pine trees, cedars, junipers ...)

... and others

Plants — 270 000 leaves on the Tree of Life

High up in tropical rainforests, the bromeliad grows into a "bowl" of leaves attached to a tree. This bowl catches water and becomes a habitat for many species of frogs, insects, spiders and worms. The largest bromeliad is just a bit smaller than a backpack. It can hold nearly 7.5 L (2 U.S. gal.) of water.

The bee orchid is an excellent mimic. Its flower looks so much like a female bee that male bees are tricked into landing on it. When they fly away, they carry pollen with them to the next flower.

Bromeliad

Milkweed

Milkweed is an important plant for monarch butterflies — it's where they lay their eggs and it's the main food for young monarch caterpillars. Eating milkweed also makes the caterpillars and butterflies poisonous to other animals.

Many plants are used in medicines. The rosy periwinkle of Madagascar is a vital ingredient in two medicines that treat cancer. Sadly, rosy periwinkles are at risk because their habitat is disappearing.

Rosy periwinkle

Bee orchid

15

Stony corals are one of many coral species that build coral reefs. These reefs are the rainforests of the ocean—they provide a habitat for a huge diversity of animals.

A fruit-eating fish? The tambaqui of the Amazon River eats fruits that fall into the water. The seeds are dispersed in the fish's waste.

Ants and acacia trees have a special relationship. Ants protect acacia trees from plant-eating insects, such as beetles and aphids. In return, the acacia tree provides nectar for the ants to eat and hollow thorns for shelter.

The Jamaican leaf-nosed bat helps spread fig seeds. The bat eats the figs, then the seeds are dispersed in the bat's droppings.

Stony coral

Tambaqui

Ant and acacia

Jamaican leaf-nosed bat

KINGDOM

Animals

1 318 000 species

From lions, tigers and bears, to jellyfish, sponges and sea slugs — the animal kingdom is by far the largest and most diverse of the five kingdoms. It accounts for about three-quarters of all leaves on the Tree of Life.

The species in this kingdom are further grouped into invertebrates (animals without backbones, such as spiders, insects, sponges and worms) and vertebrates (animals with backbones — fish, birds, reptiles, amphibians and mammals).

With or without backbones, all animals share some characteristics. Unlike plants, animals cannot create their own food. They rely on other life forms for food. Some animals (herbivores) eat plants, while others (carnivores) eat the animals that eat the plants.

Plants rely on animals, too. Most flowering plants need animals, especially insects, to take pollen from one flower to another so that new seeds can form. Without animals, many plants could not produce seeds.

Animals also help spread plant seeds. Birds and bats eat the fruit the plants produce. The fruit is digested and the seeds are dropped in the animal's waste, away from the adult plant. This gives the new plants room to grow. Even squirrels and chipmunks get into the act. They collect seeds and bury them to eat later. The seeds that are forgotten grow into new plants.

Animals even help plants grow by providing much-needed nutrients. Animal poop is a rich fertilizer.

Animal species

1 265 500 invertebrates

52 500 vertebrates

Animals — 1 318 000 leaves on the Tree of Life

Animals → Invertebrates
1 265 500 species

Invertebrates live everywhere on Earth — on land and in water. They range from sea sponges, corals and jellyfish, to insects, spiders and worms. About the only thing they all have in common is that none of them has a backbone. Instead, many have an exoskeleton — a tough, outer covering that protects them.

Of all the invertebrates, insects are probably the most familiar, for good reason — they make up more than three-quarters of all invertebrates.

Some invertebrates are enormous. The giant squid is probably the biggest invertebrate on the Tree of Life. It can grow up to 18 m (60 ft.) long and weigh over 450 kg (1000 lb.). Even its eyes are huge — as big as basketballs.

But most invertebrates are small enough that you'd easily overlook them. Their size makes them so difficult to find that scientists believe there may be millions more invertebrates still to be discovered and named.

Invertebrate species

950 000 mandibulates
(insects, centipedes, millipedes ...)

75 000 arachnids
(spiders, ticks, mites, horseshoe crabs ...)

70 000 mollusks
(snails, sea slugs, mussels, octopus, squid ...)

40 000 crustaceans
(lobsters, crabs, crayfish, shrimp, barnacles ...)

20 000 nematodes
(roundworms ...)

16 000 annelids
(leeches, earthworms ...)

9000 cnidarians
(jellyfish, corals, sea anemones ...)

7000 echinoderms
(sea stars, sea urchins, sand dollars ...)

5000 sponges

... and others

Invertebrates — 1 265 500 leaves on the Tree of Life

The nudibranch, a species of mollusk, breathes through feathery gills on its back. Sometimes called a sea slug, every nudibranch is both male *and* female.

One of the tiniest invertebrates is the tardigrade. It's smaller than a grain of salt. Under a microscope, it looks like a tiny bear, which is how it got the nickname "water bear." Tardigrades can be found all over the world, even buried in the Arctic ice.

There are 350 000 known species of beetles, including the metallic wood-boring beetle from Indonesia. In fact, there are more known species of beetles than any other group of animals on the Tree of Life.

The largest butterfly to flutter by is the Queen Alexandria birdwing butterfly. Found in New Guinea, it has a wingspan of 30 cm (12 in.) — bigger than a dinner plate. Unfortunately, its tropical habitat is being destroyed, putting these butterflies at risk.

The coconut crab is the largest land invertebrate. At 17 kg (37½ lb.), this coconut eater weighs as much as a border collie.

Dorid nudibranch

Tardigrade

Metallic wood-boring beetle

Queen Alexandria birdwing butterfly

Coconut crab

The coelacanth was thought to have been extinct for 70 million years. But in 1938, a living coelacanth was discovered, the first of many to be found. Some scientists think this deep sea fish may be an ancestor of the first land vertebrates.

If you're ever strolling through a tropical rainforest, take a look up in the trees. Maybe you will spot an emerald tree boa, one of the few reptiles that bear live young instead of laying eggs.

Coelacanth

Emerald tree boa

Strawberry poison dart frog

Imagine a frog the size of a housefly! The strawberry poison dart frog may be small, but, like all dart frogs, it is poisonous. Its bright colors warn predators to stay away.

A toco toucan's bill may look heavy, but it is actually hollow. And it is surprisingly nimble. Ridges along the edge help the toucan hold and manipulate the fruit it eats.

Toco toucan

Animals → Vertebrates
52 500 species

Vertebrates are the animals we know best. Why? Because even without a microscope, they are easy to find. All it takes is a quick look in a mirror to bring you face to face with one. But although vertebrates are all around us, they make up only a tiny portion of the species on the Tree of Life.

Vertebrates are subdivided into fish, birds, reptiles, amphibians and mammals. The main thing they have in common is a backbone, which is made up of a series of bones called vertebrae. The vertebrae house and protect the spinal cord, which works with the brain to control everything in the body. Vertebrates also have an internal skeleton that allows for movement, support and protection.

Today, vertebrates can be found on land and in water. But the first vertebrates lived only in the seas. About 360 million years ago, some of these early fish crawled out of the sea, and vertebrate life on land began.

Vertebrate species

25 100 fish
9800 birds
8000 reptiles
4960 amphibians
4640 mammals

Vertebrates —52 500 leaves on the Tree of Life

Yangtze River dolphin

Whales and dolphins, such as this Yangtze River dolphin, likely evolved from hoofed mammals. In other words, they started as land animals and moved back into the sea. Today there are only 300 Yangtze River dolphins left in the wild.

Animals →Vertebrates→Fish

25 100 species

Fish, of course, are aquatic—they spend their whole lives in the water. Most fish live in either freshwater *or* saltwater. But some, such as American eels and salmon, spend part of their life in both.

Fish are the most diverse vertebrate species. They are made up of three groups—bony fish, cartilaginous fish and jawless fish.

Bony fish are the most common. As the name suggests, they have a full skeleton made of bone. Trout, salmon, catfish and even goldfish are examples of bony fish.

Cartilaginous fish have a skeleton made of cartilage—like the stuff your nose is made of. They include sharks and rays.

Jawless fish, such as lampreys and hagfish, are the rarest and most primitive. Lampreys have a suckerlike mouth, which they use to attach themselves to other fish. They eat by scraping away the flesh of these fish with a ring of sharp teeth. Hagfish, on the other hand, are scavengers, feeding on dead and dying fish.

Most fish are cold-blooded—their body temperature is the same as their surroundings. And most have gills, and scales and fins, which help them swim.

On the Tree of Life, fish are an important food source. Many top predators, such as grizzly bears, eagles, sharks and even people, are fish eaters.

Fish species

24 150 bony fish
875 cartilaginous fish
75 jawless fish

Fish—25 100 leaves on the Tree of Life

African lungfish

The whale shark is not only the biggest shark, it's also the biggest fish in the sea. At 18 m (60 ft.) long, it is more than 100 times bigger than one of the smallest sharks—the dwarf dogshark. Surprisingly, the biggest shark eats some of the smallest life on the Tree of Life—plankton.

The clownfish lives among the poisonous tentacles of the sea anemone, but has nothing to fear. The anemone protects the clownfish from predators and, in return, gets food scraps that the fish leaves behind.

The American eel begins its life in the Sargasso Sea, near Bermuda. As it gets older, it migrates long distances to freshwater lakes, streams or coastal areas. It returns to the Sargasso Sea at the end of its life to breed.

When lakes and rivers dry up, the African lungfish buries itself in the mud and waits for rain. While buried, it uses its mouth and lungs, instead of its gills, to take in air.

Whale shark

Clownfish and sea anemone

American eel

KINGDOM
Animals →Vertebrates→Birds
9800 species

Believe it or not, birds are descendants of dinosaurs. How do we know? By comparing their skeletons. Birds have the same type of ankle joint and hips as dinosaurs. Birds are also closely related to reptiles. They have scales on their legs and their feathers likely evolved from scales, too. But unlike reptiles, birds are warm-blooded — they maintain a constant body temperature.

Besides feathers, birds' most obvious features are wings and beaks.

Wing shapes tell a lot about how birds live. Shorter wings are good for twisting through forests. Long, narrow wings are great for soaring on air currents. And flipperlike wings are ideal for diving and swimming.

A bird's beak gives clues about what it eats. Birds of prey have strong, hooked beaks to tear into their prey. Other birds have short, thick, curved beaks to crack open seeds and nuts. Nectar sippers have long, strawlike beaks.

Birds are the great migrators on the Tree of Life. Almost half of all birds migrate. Some fly great distances to and from breeding areas to escape cold climates or to find food. Migrating birds depend on many habitats along the way as resting or stopover points. Changes in even one habitat on their route can spell disaster for these migrators.

The arctic tern migrates from the North Pole to the South Pole and back again every year, a round trip of about 35 000 km (22 000 mi.).

Arctic tern

24

The gentoo penguin of the Antarctic is the bird world's fastest swimmer. It flies through the water, rather than the air, at up to 40 km/h (25 m.p.h.).

Parrots, like this Salvadori's fig parrot from Indonesia, are in trouble. Almost a third of all parrots are threatened or endangered due to habitat loss and the pet trade.

The largest living bird is the ostrich. While it can't fly, it is a great runner, reaching speeds of up to 75 km/h (47 m.p.h.).

Gentoo penguin

Salvadori's fig parrot

Ostrich

Bird species

5000 songbirds
(robins, jays, finches ...)

400 swifts and hummingbirds

330 shorebirds
(puffins, gulls, terns, sandpipers ...)

320 parrots and parakeets

290 doves

270 birds of prey
(eagles, hawks, falcons ...)

215 wading birds
(cranes, rails, coots ...)

150 waterfowl
(swans, ducks, geese ...)

135 owls

17 penguins

10 flightless birds
(ostriches, emus, rheas ...)

... and others

Birds —9800 leaves on the Tree of Life

KINGDOM

Animals →Vertebrates →Reptiles

8000 species

Slimy? No way! Reptiles actually have dry, scaly skin like their ancestors, the great dinosaurs. Their scales help trap moisture in their bodies so they don't dry out. That's why reptiles are so successful in desert habitats. But reptiles aren't just desert dwellers — they can be found in a range of habitats, from land to freshwater and even in the oceans.

Scales aren't the only thing reptiles have in common. They are also cold-blooded.

That's why they bask in the sun — to warm up. And most lay eggs rather than bear live young.

Reptiles are divided into five groups — lizards; snakes; turtles and tortoises; crocodiles, alligators and caimans; and tuatara. All play an important role in the Tree of Life as both predators and prey. Most reptiles are carnivores (animal eaters), although some lizards are herbivores (plant eaters). And then there are the omnivores, such as turtles. They eat both animals and plants.

Reptile species

4320 lizards

3300 snakes

350 turtles and tortoises

28 crocodiles, alligators and caimans

2 tuatara

Reptiles — 8000 leaves on the Tree of Life

Panther chameleon

Tuatara

Green sea turtle

African rock python

Gila monster

Tuataras, found in New Zealand, are the oldest members of the reptile family. They are directly related to the first reptiles that roamed Earth at the time of the dinosaurs. Tuataras have changed little from their ancient relatives.

The green sea turtle spends most of its life in the ocean. Every two to three years, it migrates almost 2000 km (1240 mi.) to its birth beach to mate and lay eggs. Like all sea turtles, green sea turtles are at risk.

An African rock python can grow up to 8.5 m (28 ft.) long — big enough to eat an antelope. These pythons also dine on pigs, baboons and monkeys.

Madagascar is home to almost half of the world's chameleons, including the panther chameleon. An insectivore (insect eater), the panther chameleon can flick its sticky tongue out almost twice the length of its body to grab an unsuspecting insect.

During hibernation or when food is scarce, the gila monster can live off the fat in its tail. Gila monsters are at risk and may soon become endangered due to habitat loss and the pet trade.

The Brazilian horned frog lives in the rainforests of Brazil and Argentina. A voracious eater, it will devour just about anything it can catch. It swallows food whole—including small birds, rodents and other frogs.

The female Surinam toad of South America backpacks her young. The eggs are deposited in tiny holes on her back. Her skin swells up around the eggs to protect them. And there they stay until the young toads emerge and swim away.

Most salamanders are about as long as a pen, but the Japanese giant salamander grows to ten times that length. These giants spend their whole life in water and are nocturnal (active at night). They eat crabs, fish and other small amphibians.

From water to land ... then back to water. The red-spotted newt of North America begins life in the water, metamorphoses and moves onto land. When it is old enough to breed, it moves back into the water.

Brazilian horned frog

Surinam toad

Japanese giant salamander

Animals →Vertebrates→Amphibians
4960 species

Amphibians are the only vertebrates that go through metamorphosis — the complete change from one form to another. Frogs, for example, lay their eggs in water. Tadpoles emerge from the eggs and live in the water, using their gills to breathe. As they grow, they begin to change. Lungs and legs develop. Tails shrink. When metamorphosis is complete, their lungs and legs make them ready for life on land.

There are three groups of amphibians — frogs and toads; salamanders and newts (amphibians with tails); and caecilians (legless, wormlike amphibians). Frogs and toads are by far the largest group of amphibians.

On the Tree of Life, amphibians have an important part to play. As tadpoles, they are a food source for fish, birds, reptiles, mammals and even insects, such as the larvae of dragonflies. As adults, while still prey for some animals, they also become predators. They eat insects, worms and fish. Some even eat rats and ducklings.

Amphibians are also important as indicator species (species whose health indicates the state of the environment). Their thin, slimy skin absorbs water and air, making them sensitive to both water and air pollution. They are also vulnerable to ultraviolet (UV) light. A drop in amphibian numbers is one of the first signs that something is wrong in the environment.

Amphibian species

4400 frogs and toads
400 salamanders and newts
160 caecilians

Amphibians — 4960 leaves on the Tree of Life

Red-spotted newt

Animals →Vertebrates→Mammals

4640 species

Mammals are one of the smallest groups on the Tree of Life, yet they are found in almost every environment—land, water and air. Yes, air. Bats are mammals, the only ones capable of true flight.

In size and shape, mammals are quite diverse. One of the smallest, the bumblebee bat from Thailand, weighs only about as much as two jellybeans. The largest mammal, the blue whale, weighs in at 180 t (200 tn.).

Mammals can be divided into three main groups. Most mammals are placental and give birth to live young. Some, such as kangaroos, are marsupials — they carry their young in a pouch. And then there are the monotremes, such as the echidna, or spiny anteater, which lay eggs.

What do such different mammals have in common? One thing is hair. Whether they have just a few whiskers or fur covering their entire body, all mammals have hair at some point in their life. Even dolphins have a few bristles near their snout. In most mammals, hair provides warmth. It also helps with camouflage. Spots, stripes and colors let mammals blend in with their environment or each other. Mammals also have mammary glands and feed milk to their young.

Like other species on the Tree of Life, mammals are connected by food chains and webs. Often the population (number) of one mammal species is in balance with the population of another species.

The wombat, one of the largest burrowing mammals, is slightly larger than a bulldog. This marsupial's pouch faces backward to protect its young from dirt as it burrows.

Wombat

Platypus

Sea otter

In the kelp forest, sea otters are a keystone species (species on which many others depend). Sea otters eat sea urchins and the urchins eat kelp. Kelp provides vital habitat and food for many sea creatures. Without sea otters to keep them in balance, sea urchin populations would explode and destroy the kelp forests.

At first, scientists who studied the platypus thought it was a hoax—a creature sewn together from different animals. But this unique animal is no joke. It is one of the few egg-laying mammals and also one of the few venomous mammals. The spur on the back foot of the male platypus can inject poison into a predator.

The giraffe is Earth's tallest mammal. At 5.5 m (18 ft.) tall, giraffes can reach the leaves that other herbivores can't. Even giraffe babies are tall. At just under 2 m (6.5 ft.), they are taller than most people. Despite their height, giraffes have the same number of vertebrae in their necks as all other mammals—seven.

Giraffe

Mammal species

Placental mammals such as

1814 rodents

986 bats

390 insectivores
(shrews, hedgehogs, moles ...)

240 carnivores
(dogs, cats, bears ...)

233 primates
(apes, lemurs, humans ...)

228 hoofed mammals
(pigs, zebras, hippopotamuses ...)

79 cetaceans
(dolphins, whales, porpoises ...)

69 lagomorphs
(rabbits, hares, pikas ...)

34 pinnipeds
(sea lions, seals, walruses ...)

30 toothless mammals
(anteaters, armadillos, sloths ...)

Marsupial mammals such as

70 New World opossums

54 kangaroos and wallabies

3 wombats

1 koala

Monotreme mammals such as

1 duck-billed platypus

2 echidna

... and others

Mammals—4640 leaves on the Tree of Life

Animals → Vertebrates

→ Mammals → Primates → Humans

1 species

Humans are 1 of the 233 species of primates.
We are closely related to the great apes (gorillas, orangutans and chimpanzees).

We are 1 of the 4640 species of mammals.
We have hair, mammary glands and give birth to live young, as most mammals do.

We are 1 of the 52 500 species of vertebrates.
We have a backbone to protect our spinal cord, like all other vertebrates.

We are 1 of the 1 318 000 species of animals.
We breathe air and rely directly or indirectly on plants for food, like all other animals.

Humans are 1 of the 1 750 000 species on the Tree of Life.
We are but one leaf on the Tree.

Yet, with a population of over six billion, humans have the greatest impact on the Tree of Life.

Humans — 1 leaf on the Tree of Life

Changes to the Tree of Life

The Tree of Life is constantly changing. New species are discovered every day, and known species are sometimes reclassified. Scientists think there may be as many as twenty million species on the Tree of Life.

Species are also being lost at an alarming rate. As many as 27 000 species may be lost each year — that's 74 species per day, 3 species per hour.

Every species, from fire algae to mangrove trees to zebras, needs a habitat that provides food, water and shelter. But cutting down forests, draining wetlands and plowing grasslands to build highways, roads, farms, towns and cities reduces habitat. And air, soil and water pollution threatens the quality of the habitats that remain.

🌳 The equivalent of two football fields worth of tropical rainforest are cut or burned every second to make room for pastures and farmland. Without the habitat that tropical forests provide, more than half of the world's plant and animal species may be lost.

🌳 Almost half of mangrove forests are gone — cut down for lumber or damaged by pollution, aggressive fishing and urban growth. Without mangrove forests, coastlines may slip into the ocean. Animals will lose vital habitat.

🌳 Almost a third of coral reefs have been lost due to development, overfishing and pollution. At this rate, scientists estimate that half will be gone by 2010.

🌳 Half of wetlands in the United States have been lost. Many of Canada's wetlands are also gone. Though home to an incredible diversity of species, wetlands are being drained or filled to make room for farms, houses and factories.

The extinction of even one species weakens the chain of connections among all species on the Tree of Life. Lose too many sea otters, and sea urchins will destroy the kelp forests. Lose the milkweed, and monarch caterpillars will starve. Lose plankton, and entire marine food webs will collapse.

The math is simple. The loss of habitat equals the loss of species. And the loss of even one species on the Tree of Life affects all species.

At risk

25 971 plants

1192 birds

1137 mammals

938 mollusks

752 fish

555 insects

408 species of crustaceans

296 species of reptiles

157 species of amphibians

Rainbow parrotfish

Some Species at Risk

Red panda
Maidenhair tree (gingko)
Giant clam
Fiji banded iguana
Wood poppy
Golden toad
Seaside centipede lichen
Macaroni penguin
Rainbow parrotfish
Sumatran orangutan
Lined seahorse
Chinese egret

Red panda

Maidenhair tree (gingko)

Giant clam

Wood poppy

Fiji banded iguana

Macaroni penguin

Golden toad

Seaside centipede lichen

Sumatran orangutan

Lined seahorse

Chinese egret

35

Becoming Guardians
of the Tree of Life

The Tree of Life is not here for us to prune —cut off a branch, trim a twig. It's not something we can dig up and plant somewhere else. We must learn to live our lives *within* the Tree — as 1 leaf among 1 750 000. We are part of the Tree of Life. We are its guardians, not its gardeners.

When we forget we are part of the Tree of Life, our impact can be damaging. But when we remember, it can be incredibly powerful. It doesn't take much to become a guardian of the Tree of Life. You don't need a lot of money or even a lot of time. All you need is desire, determination and the courage to think a little differently. Here are just a few simple things you can try on your own, with your family or as a class:

🌳 **Learn More**. By developing a better understanding about biodiversity and how everything is connected, you can make choices in your life that help protect the Tree of Life. Start by picking just one species from this book. Learn all you can about it. Then learn about the species that interact with your species. Then learn about the species that interact with the species that interact with your species and so on. Now take a look at things you do in your everyday life. How do your actions have an impact on these species?

🌳 **Reduce Your Impact on the Tree of Life.** Think about how you help or hinder biodiversity. Do you get a ride to school rather than walk? Cars add extra pollution to the air. Do you recycle, or turn off the lights when you leave a room? If so, you are saving resources and helping the environment, which in turn helps biodiversity. Count up all the things you do in a month that protect the Tree of Life. Try to add at least one new thing to that list every month.

🌳 **Create a Wildlife Habitat.** In a house or an apartment or even at school, you can help create habitats. Fill balcony flower boxes with plants that will attract insects and birds. Let your grass grow and add some native plant species to attract wildlife to your yard. Plant a butterfly garden in your schoolyard.

🌳 **Host a Clean-up Event.** Get your school or community group involved in cleaning up a local park or ravine. These city habitats are vital to wildlife. Invite the media and encourage community businesses to get involved, too.

🌳 **Educate Others.** Start a biodiversity club at school or in your community. Write a newsletter or host an awareness day to help others learn more about biodiversity.

Notes to Parents, Teachers and Guardians

Classification and the Tree of Life

Classification is a system of sorting and grouping living species using characteristics they have in common, such as their shape, how they move and how they reproduce and develop. Once classified, they can be assigned a place on the Tree of Life based on their connection with other species.

Taxonomy, the science of studying, identifying and classifying living organisms, has fascinated humans for thousands of years. Early on, all life was sorted into two categories — plants and animals. With the discovery of microscopes, bacteria and protoctista were observed for the first time. This led to the realization that two kingdoms were not enough. The Kingdom Monera was created containing both bacteria and protoctista.

In the mid-1950s, protoctista (celled organisms with a nucleus) were given their own kingdom. Monera remained a kingdom containing only bacteria (single-celled organisms without a nucleus). A four-kingdom system was born — plants, animals, monera and protoctista.

The current five-kingdom system was established a short time later. Fungi, though grouped with plants, are really quite unlike plants. (While plants can make their own food, fungi cannot.) Yet fungi are not animals, either. And they certainly aren't single-celled organisms. And so fungi became the fifth kingdom.

Recently, new technologies have allowed us to take a closer look at the genetic makeup of plants and animals. New discoveries are causing us to rethink former groupings. Today, scientists are looking at the possibility of dividing Monera into two kingdoms. They are also debating the role of viruses and whether they should have their own kingdom. Before long, the Tree of Life may grow to six or even seven kingdoms.

Biodiversity and the Tree of Life

Simply put, biodiversity is the incredible variety of life on Earth — from the variety of species, to the variety within species, to the variety of ecosystems (communities of living things and habitats linked together).

Most of us are aware of this diversity. We see it in our everyday life. We know about different habitats — forests, oceans, grasslands, deserts. We can recognize different species — black bears, polar bears, sun bears. And we may even be aware of differences within species — black bears can be black, brown or even cinnamon in color.

Biodiversity is not just about individual species or individual ecosystems. It's also about *how* everything on the Tree of Life interacts. Everything is interconnected in some way. Plants rely on animals for pollination; animals rely on plants for oxygen and food; and fungi and bacteria break down their waste.

Pressures on one species — or one ecosystem — can have a profound effect on all life on the Tree of Life. If these relationships are jeopardized due to loss of species or altered habitat, the damage may be dramatic and irreversible.

From a human perspective, biodiversity is vital to our existence. The potential for new foods and medicines from the natural world is huge. Only a fraction of all the plant species on the Tree of Life are currently used for food, while as many as a quarter have already proved to have medicinal value. Yet our actions are destroying species and spaces faster than we can assess their potential.

Biodiversity is important for another reason. Every leaf on the Tree of Life, every species and every individual, has its own intrinsic value, independent of any value we place on it. Most children recognize this. Many have their own inherent connection to nature. They are born with a sense of knowing that other species are alive and should be treasured. If you've ever watched young children interact with an animal or experience nature, either in a natural setting or in a museum, or even while watching a video, you've seen their eyes light up in wonder and awe. This appreciation is often lost as they grow up.

Our role as parents and teachers is to help nurture and foster this awe and to channel it toward a greater sense of awareness, responsibility and stewardship. We need to foster a *biodiversity ethic* that recognizes the diversity and interconnection of all species and the role every species plays within the Tree of Life. This biodiversity ethic will help children understand their place within the Tree, as one of its many leaves. It will help children see themselves as guardians and guide them to take actions now and as adults that conserve biodiversity and protect the Tree of Life. That's what this book is about. It's one step in helping to foster a biodiversity ethic — but the next steps are yours.

What Can You Do?

🌳 Promote the wonder of nature at home and in the classroom. Surround yourself, your family or your students with books, magazines and videos about the natural world. Take field trips to parks, conservation centers, local ravines and museums. Volunteer with an environmental group in a clean-up or fundraising event.

🌳 Incorporate biodiversity and the Tree of Life into everyday rituals. At home, invite your children into the garden with you. As you plant, talk about the life cycles of plants, seasonal changes and the relationship between plants and wildlife. Engage children in discussions about purchases, and explore more environmentally responsible choices (less packaging, recyclable containers, alternatives to chemical cleaners and pesticides and so on). In the classroom, work nature into everything you study. Math problems can revolve around numbers of species, writing projects can explore biodiversity issues, and art projects can involve nature in many ways.

🌳 Open a dialogue about nature and the environment that allows children to explore and experiment with their own thoughts and feelings. Ask them what biodiversity means to them. Pick a hot biodiversity topic and have a debate. This will help children develop their own voices and opinions on issues.

In a world that is more and more removed from nature, we have to make an extra effort to ensure our children stay connected to the natural world. Making these connections at an early age helps a child develop a lifelong passion for nature and the Tree of Life.

Index